CHANGING CONCEPTION

C000137663

The publication of the *Oxford* in September 2004 was an ev importance. In his Leslie Step...

founder of the original *Dictionary of National Biography*, the distinguished historian Keith Thomas surveys the many earlier attempts at collective biography, considers the relationship of the *Oxford DNB* to them, and offers a preliminary assessment of the *Oxford DNB* itself. The author, who has been chairman of the Supervisory Committee of the *Oxford DNB* since its inception, writes with intimate knowledge of the project. This Leslie Stephen Lecture complements the earlier Leslie Stephen and *The New Dictionary of National Biography* by the late Colin Matthew, Founder-Editor of the *Oxford DNB*, and published by Cambridge in 1997.

KEITH THOMAS is a former president of Corpus Christi College, Oxford, and of the British Academy.

KEITH THOMAS
*Fellow of All Souls College, Oxford*

# CHANGING CONCEPTIONS OF NATIONAL BIOGRAPHY: THE *OXFORD DNB* IN HISTORICAL PERSPECTIVE

Leslie Stephen Special Lecture
*Delivered in the Senate House,*
*Cambridge, 1 October 2004*

**CAMBRIDGE**
UNIVERSITY PRESS

CAMBRIDGE UNIVERSITY PRESS
Cambridge, New York, Melbourne, Madrid,
Cape Town, Singapore, São Paulo

CAMBRIDGE UNIVERSITY PRESS
The Edinburgh Building, Cambridge, CB2 2RU, UK
Published in the United States of America
by Cambridge University Press, New York

www.cambridge.org
Information on this title: www.cambridge.org/9780521671187

First published 2005

Printed in the United Kingdom at the University Press, Cambridge

*A catalogue record for this book is available from the British Library*

ISBN-13 978-0-521-67118-7 paperback
ISBN-10 0-521-67118-3 paperback

# CHANGING CONCEPTIONS OF NATIONAL BIOGRAPHY: THE *OXFORD DNB* IN HISTORICAL PERSPECTIVE

The Leslie Stephen Special Lecture by
Sir Keith Thomas
*Fellow of All Souls College, Oxford*
*Delivered in the Senate House, Cambridge*
*1 October 2004*

ॐ

Sir Leslie Stephen was the founding editor of the *Dictionary of National Biography* (*DNB*) and this is not the first of the lectures commemorating his name to be concerned with that great enterprise. It is an honour to stand where Stephen's co-editor and successor, Sir Sidney Lee, lectured in 1911 on 'Principles of Biography', and where, only nine years ago, Colin Matthew, founding editor of the *Oxford Dictionary of National Biography*, outlined the project whose publication we celebrate today.

As chairman of the Supervisory Committee of the *Oxford DNB*, I had the privilege of being in almost daily contact with Colin Matthew when the *Dictionary* was being planned. I have remained in close touch with his successor, Brian Harrison, and the project director, Robert Faber, and I am grateful to them both for help in connection with this lecture.

Stephen's *DNB* was nothing if not heroic, in conception and execution. Between 1885 and 1900 sixty-three volumes rolled off the press at quarterly intervals. They contained the lives of over 29,000 people and they became the international benchmark against which all other attempts at national biography would be measured. Now, a century later, we have in the *Oxford DNB* a work which, at 62.5 million words, is nearly twice the size of its predecessor, and produced in two thirds of the time; a collective achievement, in which all involved can take justifiable pride.

These two great monuments of learning can only be understood if they are seen as the culmination of several centuries of biographical effort; and, if only to moderate any tendency to excessive triumphalism on this occasion, I should like to begin by reminding you of what the *Oxford DNB* owes to its predecessors, before reflecting on the new work itself.

Collective biography was a long-established practice when Stephen began his work. Typically, it took one of three forms: group biography, universal biography and national biography. The first of these, group biography, was a classical genre, exemplified in such works as Cornelius Nepos's lives of generals and Suetonius's lives of Caesars, and much practised in Renaissance Italy, with collected lives of popes, writers, artists and military leaders.[1] It became a common literary genre throughout Europe, and in eighteenth-century Britain there were scores of collected biographies, whether of actors, admirals, bishops, botanists, dramatists, Gresham professors, learned women, physicians, poets or regicides. One obvious impulse behind this kind of writing was the desire of emerging professional groups to establish a pedigree for themselves. Another was the attempt of competing religious denominations to construct their own heroic canon. In the eighteenth century, ejected clergy, both Anglican and Nonconformist, Catholic martyrs and persecuted Quakers all had their collective biographies.[2]

Some were works of what we would call scholarship. If we exclude John Foxe's Protestant martyrology, as not strictly biographical in character, the first carefully

[1] See, e.g., *Modelling the Individual: Biography and Portrait in the Renaissance*, ed. Karl Enenkel, Betsy de Jong-Crane and Peter Liebregis (Amsterdam and Atlanta, GA, 1998), pp. 11, 33–4.

[2] A useful list of these works can be found in the *Bibliographical Supplement* to Donald A. Stauffer, *The Art of Biography in Eighteenth-Century England* (Princeton, NJ, 1941). See also Pat Rogers, 'Johnson's *Lives of the Poets* and the Biographic Dictionaries', *Review of English Studies*, new ser., 31 (1980). The most important of their European counterparts are listed in the Preface to Louis Moréri, *Le Grand Dictionnaire Historique* (Utrecht, Leyden and Amsterdam, 1692), sigs. A2–4v. On the polemical motivation of collective biography in eighteenth-century France, see Daniel A. Bell, *The Cult of the Nation in France: Inventing Nationalism, 1680–1800* (Cambridge, MA, 2001), pp. 126, 128–39.

researched group biography in English was Anthony Wood's account of Oxford writers, *Athenae Oxonienses* (1691–2). Wood was highly partisan. He wrote to advance the honour of the University of Oxford, by showing the contribution its members had made to learning; and his Royalist prejudices were tendentiously expressed. But he was meticulous in his efforts to establish the precise dates of the key events in the lives of his subjects. He searched parish registers and institutional archives, and conducted an extensive correspondence. Though arranged chronologically rather than alphabetically, his lives were in many ways authentic forerunners of the *DNB*-style notice. The *Oxford DNB*'s entry on Wood remarks that without his biographical records, 'half the seventeenth-century entries in the *DNB* could hardly have been written'. In the sources, *Athenae Oxonienses* is cited 1,464 times.

The second kind of biographical enterprise was universal biography. The idea of collecting the lives of all the notable people who had ever lived was formulated by the scholarly polymaths of early modern Europe, who sought to classify and organise knowledge at a time when the printing revolution was producing a deluge of undigested information. They did so by compiling vast encyclopaedic dictionaries of literary, historical and geographical learning. The first great international success was *Le Grand Dictionnaire Historique* (1673) by the

French priest, Louis Moréri, which, expanded by others, grew until it filled ten folio volumes. After it, came the great eighteenth-century encyclopaedias: Diderot and d'Alembert in France, Zedler and Brockhaus in Germany, *Encyclopaedia Britannica* in Scotland. Many of these works had a biographical element, but the Huguenot Pierre Bayle's *Dictionnaire Historique et Critique* (1697) was distinctive in being organised biographically and backed up by a crushing weight of documentation, with footnotes on the page, footnotes on footnotes, and sometimes footnotes on footnotes on footnotes. In one of the two rival English translations of this work (1734–41), the editors inserted an additional 900 British lives, most of them well documented and written by the phenomenally industrious antiquarian, Thomas Birch, whose role in the development of British biography is crucial.[3]

Thereafter, there were several English attempts at compiling universal biography in the continental

[3] (Pierre Bayle), *A General Dictionary, Historical and Critical*, trans and ed. John Peter Bernard, Thomas Birch, John Lockman and others (1734–41). Birch's work has been plausibly hailed as 'the first important ancestor of the *Dictionary of National Biography*' and (forgetting Anthony Wood) 'the first attempt in England to apply the inductive method to biography'; James Marshall Osborn, 'Thomas Birch and the *General Dictionary* (1734–41)', *Modern Philology*, 36 (1938–9): 25.

manner.[4] The results were largely derivative in content, but they helped to develop collected concise biography as an art form. The *New and General Biographical Dictionary*, put out by a group of booksellers in 1761, was efficiently presented, and went into several later editions, culminating in that of 1812–17, when the industrious Alexander Chalmers added nearly 4,000 lives, rewrote over 2,000 and revised the rest, making a grand total of over 9,000 lives in 32 volumes. This became the standard English-language universal biography, despite competition from the ten volumes of John Aikin's *General Biography* (1799–1815) and the twelve volumes of the *New General Biographical Dictionary* (1839–48), planned by the High Churchman Hugh James Rose and seen through by his brother Henry John and the antiquary Thomas Wright. The Roses' first six volumes made a stately progress from 'A' to 'C', the second six scampered from 'D' to 'Z'.

---

[4] 'Biographical Dictionaries', in *Selected Essays and Papers of Richard Copley Christie*, ed. William A. Shaw (1902), remains a valuable survey. A more recent account is Isabel Rivers, 'Biographical Dictionaries and their Uses from Bayle to Chalmers', in *Books and their Readers in Eighteenth-Century England: New Essays*, ed. Isabel Rivers (2001).

Sidney Lee would dismiss both Rose and Chalmers as 'inadequate',[5] but he made no mention of the much more ambitious venture by the Society for the Diffusion of Useful Knowledge, which, under pressure from its President, Lord Brougham, embarked in 1842 on their *Biographical Dictionary*. It never got beyond the letter 'A', because it bankrupted the Society. But in quality it surpassed all its predecessors. It used standard sources to give 'some account of all persons who have lived and done anything for which they ought to be remembered';[6] and it did so in a concise, unvarnished way, with authorities cited at the end of each notice. Its contributors came from Europe as well as Britain and were mostly based in universities or museums. Leslie Stephen said that its English lives offered the best existing model for the *DNB*.[7] Had the project been completed, it would have occupied some 150 volumes. As it is, the seven volumes devoted to letter 'A' lie in

[5] 'A Statistical Account', Preface to volume I of 1908 edition of *D[ictionary of] N[ational] B[iography]*, ed. Leslie Stephen and Sidney Lee, p. vi. For devastating criticism of Rose, see Bolton Corney, *On the New General Biographical Dictionary* (1839).

[6] The Society for the Diffusion of Useful Knowledge, *Biographical Dictionary* (1842–44), vol. 1 (1), p. v.

[7] 'A New *Biographia Britannica*', *The Athenaeum* (23 Dec. 1882), p. 850. It included some British figures who do not appear in the *Oxford DNB*.

the stacks of the Bodleian Library, some still awaiting the paper knife.

In Britain, universal biography never got beyond more or less competent syntheses of existing knowledge. In France, by contrast, the encyclopaedic tradition launched by Moréri and Bayle generated a series of increasingly formidable works, culminating in two stupendous monuments. From 1810 onwards, the bookseller, Louis-Gabriel Michaud, aided by 300 specialist collaborators, many of great distinction, produced a *Biographie Universelle*, markedly royalist and antirevolutionary in tone, but, in the forty-five volumes of its second edition (1842–65), impressive enough to achieve world supremacy in the genre, despite a strong challenge, involving litigation, from its rival, the *Nouvelle Biographie Générale* from the publishers Firmin Didot, in forty-six volumes (1852–66).[8]

French domination in the field of universal biography caused much irritation on this side of the Channel,

[8] The first edition of *Biographie Universelle* was published between 1810 and 1828, in 52 volumes, subsequently extended to 84. On the two editions, see E[rnest] D[esplaces], in *Biographie Universelle (Michaud)*, new edn (Paris, 1842–65), vol. xxviii, p. 215n. For the litigation, see *ibid.*, vol. xii, pp. ix–xxvii; vol. xii, pp. v–li; vol. xxviii, p. 216n; and for the two dictionaries in general, *Selected Essays and Papers of Richard Copley Christie*, pp. 24–50.

particularly as the *Biographie Universelle* seemed to contain a superfluity of obscure Frenchmen, while being very weak on the British. 'Think of the difference between our books of reference and those of the French', lamented Matthew Arnold in 1864, 'between our biographical dictionaries (to take a striking instance) and theirs.'[9] It is easy to understand why it was a new universal biography, to supersede the French ones, which Leslie Stephen's munificent publisher, George Smith, wanted him to edit, until Stephen persuaded him that the project was too ambitious and that he should opt for a national dictionary instead.

This third category, national biography, was closely related to the emergence of nationalist sentiment. As Ernest Renan famously observed, every nation needs

[9] 'The Literary Influence of Academies', *Essays by Matthew Arnold* (Oxford, 1914), p. 47. Samuel Johnson observed in 1773 that 'we have no such book as Moréri's dictionary'; *Boswell's Life of Johnson*, ed. George Birkbeck Hill, revd L. F. Powell (Oxford, 1934–50), vol. xxxi. In 1839 Bolton Corney, at the end of his essay, *On the New General Biographical Dictionary: A Specimen of Amateur Criticism*, announced that he was bringing out a work entitled *Details on British Biography*, which would include a chapter, 'On the Comparative Urgency of a General Biography, and a British Biography'. In 1851 Thomas Carlyle called for an English version of the *Biographie Universelle*, in which the British lives would be better done; *The Life of John Stirling*, in *Works* (1896–9), vol. xi, p. 138.

its great men and its heroic past.[10] It also needs a literary canon. In sixteenth-century England, the antiquaries, John Leland and John Bale, compiled lists of English medieval writers and their works, in order to 'advance the honour of the realm' by showing how many learned persons their country had produced.[11] In the seventeenth and early eighteenth centuries, the same task was attempted for Scotland by Thomas Dempster and George Mackenzie, and for Ireland by Sir James Ware.[12] Although they listed many writers who

[10] Ernest Renan, *Qu'est-ce qu'une nation?* (1882), trans. in *Becoming National: A Reader*, ed. Geoffrey Eley and Ronald Grigor Suny (New York and Oxford, 1996), p. 52.

[11] Anthony Wood, *Athenae Oxonienses*, ed. Philip Bliss (1813–20), vol. i, p. 198; Cathy Shrank, *Writing the Nation in Reformation England 1530–1580* (Oxford, 2004), pp. 18, 23, 65, 69–70, 103. Trevor Roos, 'Dissolution and the Making of the English Literary Canon: the Catalogues of Leland and Bale', *Renaissance and Reformation*, new ser. 15 (1991), p. 58, points out that Leland and Bale worked within a tradition of medieval cataloguing going back to St Jerome and that their immediate inspiration was the work of the German, Johannes Trithemius, *Liber de Scriptoribus Ecclesiasticis* (1494), and the Swiss, Conrad Gesner, *Bibliotheca Universalis* (1545).

[12] Thomas Dempster, *Historia Ecclesiastica Gentis Scotorum* (Bologna, 1627); George Mackenzie, *The Lives and Characters of the Most Eminent Writers of the Scots Nation* (Edinburgh, 1708–22); James Ware, *De Scriptoribus Hiberniae* (Dublin, 1639). On collective biography in Ireland, see C. J. Woods, 'A Guide to Irish Biographical Dictionaries', *The Maynooth Review*, 6 (1980).

never existed, these authors initiated the genre of bio-bibliography, which culminated in Thomas Tanner's *Bibliotheca Britannico-Hibernica* (1748), and explains why the old *DNB* felt it necessary to append to each entry a list of its subject's writings.

The first attempt at a national biography was Thomas Fuller's *Worthies of England* (1662). Based on much research, literary and oral, it was arranged on a county-by-county basis, and interspersed with topographical and miscellaneous information. Though anecdotal, unsystematic, naively patriotic and unduly anxious not to be boring, Fuller recorded many lives which had never previously been written. The *Oxford DNB* cites him as a source 139 times.[13]

Much more ambitious was the *Biographia Britannica*, published between 1747 and 1766 in 4,600 pages,

---

[13] There is an excellent account of Fuller by William Oldys in *Biographia Britannica* (1747–66), vol. iii, and a recent appreciation in Ian Donaldson, 'National Biography and the Arts of Memory: From Thomas Fuller to Colin Matthew', in *Mapping Lives: The Uses of Biography*, ed. Peter France and William St Clair (Oxford: British Academy, 2002). Fuller had been preceded by several earlier and scrappier compilations: Henry Holland, *Heroologia Anglicana* (1620), contained short Latin lives of English notables since the time of Henry VIII; and William Winstanley, *England's Worthies: Select Lives of the Most Eminent Persons* (1660), went from the Emperor Constantine to Oliver Cromwell.

in seven folio volumes, and declaring itself 'a British Temple of Honour, sacred to the piety, learning, valour, public spirit, loyalty and every other glorious virtue of our ancestors'. It aimed to include all those who 'by their performances of any kind deserve to be remembered'.[14] The contributors were a group of antiquarians, led by William Oldys, and including Philip Nichols, an ex-Fellow of Trinity Hall, who had been expelled for stealing books from Cambridge libraries.[15] Their model was Bayle's *Dictionary*, with lengthy footnotes and copious, ill-digested excerpts from the works of the subjects. In 1778 a greatly enlarged second edition was begun under the editorship of the Presbyterian minister, Andrew Kippis (Dr Johnson having declined the post). By 1795 there were five volumes (reaching 'F' for 'Fastolf'). But Kippis's death, followed by a fire in the publisher's warehouse, brought an end to the project.

[14] *Biographia Britannica* (1747–66), vol. i, p. viii.

[15] A key to the identity of the contributors (who signed with a single letter of the alphabet) is provided in vol. i of the 2nd edn, ed. Andrew Kippis (1778–95), p. xx. See also *The Gentleman's Magazine* (1779), pp. 173, 288, 489. On Oldys, see Bolton Corney, *Curiosities of Literature by I. D'Israeli, Esq.* (2nd edn, 1838), pp. 176–80, and *Notes and Queries*, 3rd ser., i (1862), 62–3; and, on Nichols, Owen Chadwick, 'The Case of Philip Nichols, 1733', *Trans. Cambridge Bibliographical Soc.*, vol. i (1949–57).

The nationalist intentions of the *Biographia Britannica* were undisguised. It sought to advance 'the reputation of our country' and 'the honour of our ancestors' by showing how many valuable figures Britain had produced in every field of knowledge.[16] The literary counterpart of the emerging national pantheon in Westminster Abbey,[17] the *Biographia Britannica* was one of a remarkable cluster of cultural manifestations of British nationalism in the mid-eighteenth century, like the British Museum (1753), Johnson's *Dictionary* (1755), Horace Walpole's *Anecdotes of English Painting* (1762–4), the Royal Academy (1768), the *Encyclopaedia Britannica* (1768), James Granger's biographical catalogue of historical portraits (1769), and Thomas Warton's history of English poetry (1774).[18]

Accorded the rare honour of prompt translation into German,[19] the *Biographia Britannica* remained the

---

[16] *Biographia Britannica*, vol. i, p. xv; *Biographia Britannica*, 2nd edn, ed. Kippis, vol. iii, Preface.

[17] Where places could be bought from the Dean and Chapter; Matthew Craske, 'Westminster Abbey 1720–70; A Public Pantheon Built upon Private Interest', in *Pantheons: Transformations of a Monumental Idea*, ed. Richard Wrigley and Matthew Craske (Aldershot, 2004).

[18] See Gerald Newman, *The Rise of English Nationalism: A Cultural History 1740–1830* (1987), p. 112.

[19] *Samlung von merkwürdigen Lebensbeschreibungen grösten Theils aus der britannischen Biographie*, trans. and ed. Siegmund Jacob Baumgarten (Halle, 1754–7).

standard national biography for another century. Though unalluring in format, it embodied much research, contained some enormous articles (including nearly 150 pages on Captain Cook) and gave full references to sources. In the 1850s the publisher John Murray considered revising the whole work, under the editorship of William Smith, a famous producer of learned dictionaries, but was frightened off by the likely cost.[20] When the baton eventually passed to Leslie Stephen, he called his project 'a new *Biographia Britannica*'.[21]

By then, that work was a hundred years old and Britain, after being first in the race for a national biography, was now visibly lagging behind. Stephen's venture was applauded because it would at last remove 'the stigma of not possessing a national biographical dictionary'.[22] During the course of the nineteenth century such works had become an obligatory accompaniment to the process of European state formation. Collected lives of national heroes, along with portraits and statues, were a stock way of forging national identity and generating national pride. Between 1834 and 1845 Emilio de Tipaldo compiled ten volumes on illustrious

[20] (Leonard Huxley), *The House of Smith Elder* (1923), p. 18.
[21] *The Athenaeum*, 23 Dec. 1882.
[22] H. S. Ashbee in *The Athenaeum*, 2880 (6 Jan. 1883), p. 17.

Italians, in order to assert the claims of what he, rather prematurely, called '[la] nazione italiana'.[23] The first European country to complete a full-scale national biography was Sweden, with twenty-three volumes between 1835 and 1857.[24] Then came the Netherlands, with twenty-one volumes between 1852 and 1878. Austria (after several false starts) and Belgium began in the 1860s, Germany (particularly impressively) in 1875, Denmark in 1887. In the United States, there were several attempts, starting in the 1790s with Jeremy Belknap's *American Biography*, and culminating in the 1880s with the six volumes of *Appleton's Cyclopaedia of American Biography*.

All these compilations had an unconcealed nationalist agenda, from the Belgian dictionary, initiated in

[23] *Biografia degli Italiani Illustri nelle Scienze, Lettere ed Arti del Secolo XVIIII, e de' Contemporanei* (Venice, 1834–45), i, p. viii.

[24] *Biographiskt Lexicon öfver namnkunnige Svenska män*, ed. V. F. Palmblad (Uppsala, 1835–57). Including persons who were still alive, but excluding the pre-Reformation period, it built on a shorter biographical dictionary compiled fifty years earlier by the pastor, Georg Gezelius: *Försök til et Biographiskt Lexicon öfver namnkunnige och lärde Svenske män* (Stockholm and Uppsala, 1778–87), which contained 600 entries for individuals who lived between 1521 and 1771. (For assistance with Swedish sources, I am indebted to Barbara Howes, Curator of Scandinavian Books at the British Library, and to Elizabeth Baigent, former Research Director of the *Oxford DNB*.)

1845 by a royal decree when the 'Belgian nation' was only fourteen years old,[25] to Richard Ryan's *Biographia Hibernica* (1821), whose Preface, dedicated to 'the Irish nation', appealed to biography 'as the vindicator of an unhappy people'. Colin Matthew used to say that every Irish rebel of 1798 seemed to have been included in the *DNB* because Leslie Stephen, a strong Liberal Unionist, was anxious to stress that the Irish were part of British history. But a more immediate explanation was that in the seven volumes of R. R. Madden's *The United Irishmen, their Lives and Times* (1843–6) he had a copious source of information to hand.[26]

Right up to the present day, dictionaries of national biography have retained a preoccupation with creating national unity out of disparate ingredients. The Australian and New Zealand enterprises are particularly self-conscious about their role in this respect, while a recent volume of the *Dictionary of Canadian Biography* expresses the hope that 'all Canadians, to whatever

[25] *Biographie Nationale publié par l'Académie Royale* (Brussels, 1866–1944), vol. i, pp. xi–xiii.

[26] Colin Matthew, *Leslie Stephen and the New Dictionary of National Biography* (Leslie Stephen Lecture, Cambridge, 1997), p. 13. Madden is cited seventy-two times in the *Oxford D[ictionary of] N[ational] B[iography] in Association with the British Academy]*, ed. H. C. G. Matthew and Brian Harrison (Oxford, 2004).

ethnic or social group they belong and whatever their place of origin or religious beliefs, may glean from these pages the historical sustenance so necessary for creating their identity'.[27]

Yet state consolidation was not the only purpose served by national biography in the years before the *DNB*. Since classical times, the commemoration of the virtuous dead had been seen as a moral duty and an incentive to their emulation by the living. Just as Plutarch's *Parallel Lives* exemplified virtue and vice in the lives of great men, so, in the Middle Ages, socially important values were transmitted through tales of warriors, distinguished for their bravery, and saints for their spirituality. In Renaissance Italy there were numerous compilations 'Of Famous Men' (*De Viris Illustribus*), serving this exemplary purpose. In England, the illustrious were called 'worthies', whether, for Fuller, *Worthies of England* or, for John Prince in 1701, *Worthies of Devon*, or, for Montagu Burrows in 1874, *Worthies of All Souls*. Like most eighteenth-century biography, the *Biographia Britannica* was firmly in this exemplary tradition, emphasising 'the vast importance of setting worthy examples before the eyes of posterity', and holding out

[27] *Dictionary of Canadian Biography*, ed. George W. Brown *et al.* (Toronto, 1966–), vol. xiv, pp. vii–viii.

the enticing possibility that those readers who followed
these examples might themselves be included in later
volumes.[28]

Naturally, the choice of lives to be commemorated
depended on the values to be inculcated. Clement
Barksdale's *Characters and Historical Memorials ...
of England's Late Worthies* (1662) sought to reconcile
Nonconformists to the Church of England by recall-
ing the 'excellent men and women' who had belonged
to it.[29] Conversely, John Howie, a stern upholder of the
covenanting tradition, published his *Scots Worthies* in
1775 because he believed that an age of apostasy and
backsliding needed to be reminded of 'useful, holy and
exemplary lives'.[30] Thomas Birch's biographies of sev-
enteeenth-century figures in Bayle's *Dictionary* reflected
a strong personal commitment to the good old cause.
He went on to edit the works of Milton and the state
papers of Cromwell's secretary, Thurloe. Many of the
collective biographers of the later eighteenth century

---

[28] *Biographia Britannica*, vol. i, p. xv (and p. viii).
[29] Clement Barksdale, *Characters, and Historical Memorials, in
the Lives and Actions of England's Late Worthies, in Church and
State* (1662), 'To the Reader'.
[30] [John Howie of Lochgoin], *Biographia Scoticana; or a Brief
Historical Account of ... the Most Eminent Scots Worthies*, 3rd edn
(Edinburgh, 1796), Preface, p. vi.

were dissenting ministers, nominally Presbyterians, but actually Unitarians, with radical and free-thinking sympathies. Joseph Towers, who published seven volumes of well-researched *British Biography* (1766–72) was a member of the Constitutional Society and a 'citizen of the world'.[31] John Aikin, editor of *General Biography*, was a radical with a Dissenting background; he regarded the canal engineer, James Brindley, as a greater hero than Alexander the Great.[32] John Platts, the first five volumes of whose *A New Universal Biography* were published in 1825, was a Unitarian minister. Andrew Kippis, in Boswell's opinion, revised the *Biographia Britannica* 'judiciously . . . and with more impartiality than might have been expected from a Separatist'; even so, it was 'too much crowded with obscure dissenting teachers'.[33] On the Reverend James Granger's *Biographical History*, Dr Johnson was more forthright: 'The dog is a

---

[31] Joseph Towers, *British Biography* (1766–72); James Lindsay, *A Sermon, Occasioned by the Death of the Rev. Joseph Towers* (1799), pp. 34–5, 54.

[32] John Aikin *et al.*, *General Biography* (1799–1815), vol. i, Preface, p. 4.

[33] A judgement he later retracted; *Boswell's Life of Johnson*, vol. iii, p. 174 and n. 3. In 1784 Bishop Hurd described Kippis's *Biographia Britannica* as 'full of the nonsense and impertinence of these people'; Francis Kilvert, *Memoirs of the Life and Writings of the Right Rev. Richard Hurd* (1860), p. 152.

Whig ... I hate to see a Whig in a parson's gown.'[34] Most guardians of the temple of fame had a distinctive agenda.

Yet they also sought, in Fuller's words, 'to entertain the reader with delight'.[35] Hence Leslie Stephen's hope that the *DNB* would turn out to be 'one of the most amusing books in the language'.[36] Gossip about other people is doubtless an ancient activity, but it reached its apotheosis in Hanoverian Britain, where an enormous variety of clubs and voluntary associations provided a context in which the chattering classes could talk about each other. The mental habits generated in this world of public sociability encouraged the biographical way of thinking. The reclusive Anthony Wood remarked how ironic it was that his *Athenae* had not been produced by 'one who frequents much society in common rooms ... coffee houses, assignations, clubs, &c, where the characters of men and their works are frequently discussed'.[37] Two centuries later, the *DNB* and its early supplements were rooted in the world of gentlemen's clubs, that 'tight London-based elite, with

[34] *Boswell's Life of Johnson*, vol. v, p. 255.
[35] Thomas Fuller, *The History of the Worthies of England*, new edn by P. Austin Nuttall (1840), vol. i, p. 1.
[36] Leslie Stephen, 'National Biography', in *Studies of a Biographer* (1898–1902), vol. i, p. 12.
[37] Wood, *Athenae Oxonienses*, ed. Bliss, vol. i, p. clvi.

all its wealth of confidential information and taste for mutual assessment'.[38] These sociable milieux hatched a fascination with individual lives and personality.

Particularly striking was the taste for obituaries, like those in the *Gentleman's Magazine*, and for anecdotes, the subject of numerous books, most famously John Nichols's monumental *Literary Anecdotes of the Eighteenth Century*, which the *Oxford DNB* cites as a source on over 600 occasions. Here we see the origins of what the *DNB* would more grandly call 'personal knowledge and private information'. When, in 1892, Frederic Boase embarked on his remarkable *Modern English Biography*, which would contain notices of 30,000 people who died between 1851 and 1900, he planned to include 'anyone who has been well known and about whom a question might arise in general conversation'.[39] Collective biography presupposed a social encounter where someone might pause in the midst of conversation and cross the room to take down a book and check a fact.[40]

[38] Brian Harrison, 'A Slice of their Lives: Editing the *D.N.B.*, 1882–1999', *English Historical Review*, 119 (2004): 1186.

[39] Frederic Boase, *Modern English Biography* (Truro, 1892–1921; 1956 reprint), Preface to the first edition.

[40] Louis Simond described the distinctively English taste for biography as 'the gossiping of clever people'; *Journal of a Tour and Residence in Great Britain, during the Years 1810 and 1811 by a French Traveller* (Edinburgh, 1815), vol. i, p. 187.

This kind of sociability may also explain the readiness with which extreme individuality, not to say eccentricity, was hailed as a sign of national health. Britain, it was said, had more 'characters' and 'originals' than other nations because of its exceptional tolerance and freedom. 'We are ... more unlike one another than any nation I know', boasted Sir William Temple in 1690.[41] This taste for eccentricity explains the remarkable inclusiveness of some of these early biographical compilations. Fuller set the pattern when he included in his *Worthies* those who were 'over, under, or beside the standard of common persons, for strength, stature, fruitfulness, vivacity, or any other observable eminence'. He even included 'mechanics who in any manual trade have reached a clear note above others in their vocation'.[42] In the eighteenth century pirates, gamblers and highwaymen were regarded as fit subjects for collective biography no less than scholars

---

[41] *Critical Essays of the Seventeenth Century*, ed. J. E. Spingarn (Oxford, 1909), vol. iii, p. 105. Also Richard Steele in *The Guardian*, 144 (26 Aug. 1713) and Paul Langford, *Englishness Identified: Manners and Character 1650–1850* (Oxford, 2000), pp. 290–300.

[42] Fuller, *Worthies*, vol. i, p. 55.

and poets.[43] In his *Biographical History*, Granger divided his subjects hierarchically into twelve classes. The bottom class comprised 'persons of both sexes, chiefly of the lowest order of the people, remarkable from only one circumstance in their lives; namely such as lived to a great age, deformed persons, convicts, &c'.[44] If we want to know why Stephen's *DNB* contained brothel-keepers, contortionists, gamblers, transvestites and centenarians, it is to this tradition that we should look.

[43] 'Captain Alexander Smith', *The History of the Lives of the Most Noted Highwaymen* (1714; and later edns); 'Captain Charles Johnson', *A General History of the Robberies and Murders of the Most Notorious Pyrates* (1724; 4th edn, 1726) (the two works were combined in 'Captain Charles Johnson', *The General History of the Lives and Adventures of the Most Famous Highwaymen, Murderers, Street Robbers, &c* (1734)); Theophilus Lucas, *The Memoirs of the Lives, Intrigues, and Comical Adventures of the Most Famous Gamesters and Celebrated Sharpers* (1714).

[44] J(ames) Granger, *A Biographical History of England from Egbert the Great to the Revolution* (1769); continued by Mark Noble, *A Biographical History of England from the Revolution to the End of George I's Reign* (1806). On the inclusiveness of this pictorial tradition, see Marcia Pointon, *Hanging the Head: Portraiture and Social Formation in Eighteenth-Century England* (New Haven, CT, and London, 1993), pp. 53–78, 85–94. Other works catering for the taste for eccentricity were James Caulfield, *Portraits, Memoirs and Characters of Remarkable Persons* (1794–5) and R. S. Kirby, *Kirby's Wonderful and Eccentric Museum* (1803–20).

There was also a more ambitious purpose behind some of these eighteenth-century compilations. It was an Enlightenment belief that the study of individual lives could enable one to arrive at a science of human psychology. Edmund Calamy hoped in 1702 that his biographies of ejected Nonconformist ministers would assist 'the better understanding of human nature'.[45] In the *Biographia Britannica* Kippis claimed that collective biography presented 'a variety of events that, like experiments in natural philosophy, may become the materials from which general truths and principles are to be drawn'. Biography was thus elevated 'to the dignity of science; and of such science as must ever be esteemed of peculiar importance, because it hath Man for its object'.[46] One effect of this doctrine, as Dr Johnson pointed out, was to make the life of almost *any* individual worth studying. Indeed, the more ordinary the person, the more instructive the life, since most readers would find it closer to their own experience.[47] At the end of his *Biographical History*, Granger paused: 'I have,

[45] A. G. Matthews, *Calamy Revised* (Oxford, 1934), p. xviii.
[46] *Biographia Britannica* (2nd edn), vol. i, p. xxi.
[47] *The Rambler*, 60 (13 Oct. 1750); *The Idler*, 84 (24 Nov. 1759). Thomas Sprat had expressed the same view in 1668; 'The Life of Abraham Cowley', Preface to *The Poetical Works of Abraham Cowley* (Edinburgh, 1777), vol. i, p. xl.

perhaps ... extended the sphere of it too far: I began with monarchs, and have ended with ballad-singers, chimney-sweepers and beggars.' But he reassured himself: in their bodies and minds there was no difference between a king and the meanest of his subjects.[48]

So when Leslie Stephen embarked on the *DNB*, he had a long tradition on which to draw. The idea of an alphabetically organised dictionary of national biography had been familiar since the *Biographia Britannica*. The names of those to go into it were largely provided by earlier compilations, many of them notable for their broad inclusiveness; Stephen thought that all names in the old collections had a prescriptive right to inclusion.[49] The basic format of a *DNB* life, with its distinctive aesthetic of elegant condensation, giving the maximum amount of information in the minimum of space, had been successively refined by Towers, Aikin and Chalmers and was admirably exemplified in the dictionary begun by the Society for the Diffusion of Useful Knowledge. The notion that entries should vary in length with the subject's importance had been proclaimed by the *Nouvelle Biographie Générale*. The insistence on documented precision went back to Anthony

---

[48] *A Biographical History of England*, vol. ii, p. 567.
[49] *Studies of a Biographer*, vol. i, p. 15.

Wood and Thomas Birch; and the need for a biographical 'catechism' as an *aide-mémoire* to the construction of an entry, comparable to the *Oxford DNB*'s *Notes for Contributors*, had been recognised in the eighteenth century by Richard Rawlinson, when revising Wood's *Athenae*, and by Andrew Kippis in the *Biographia Britannica*.[50]

The *DNB* did not go out of its way to acknowledge its debt to its predecessors, perhaps because it so clearly excelled them in scholarship, editorial coherence and relative impartiality. Tranquil consciousness of Britain's world superiority made it less obviously chauvinistic than its European counterparts, for whom national independence was newer and less secure; it could afford to dispense with a Preface in which nationalist sentiments might have been expressed. Like several other late nineteenth-century publications, the *DNB* fostered the notion of a shared national culture transcending differences of class and region.[51] But it did so in a subtle way. Stephen drew his entries from a broad constituency,

[50] *Nouvelle Biographie Générale* (Paris, 1855–66), vol. i, p. 1; *Boswell's Life of Johnson*, vol. iv, pp. 376, 548. In addition, reference to 'private information' as the source for an entry can be found in Aikin, *General Biography*, vol. iv, p. 162.

[51] John L. Kijinski, 'John Morley's "English Men of Letters" Series and the Politics of Reading', *Victorian Studies*, 34 (1991).

comprising the British Isles and the colonies. He also followed the example of several European dictionaries in including foreigners who had played a part in British life and British nationals who had been active abroad.[52]

Only when the venture was complete did the jingoism appear. Stephen's contemporaries were delighted that the *DNB* had surpassed all its rivals. The *Pall Mall Gazette* claimed it was 'the best dictionary of home biography possessed by any nation';[53] and the *Athenaeum* said that the British had administered 'a handsome beating to their most formidable competitor, the Germans'.[54] The fact that the *DNB* had been privately financed, rather than state supported, like most of the European dictionaries, was hailed as proof of British self-reliance.[55]

[52] Lee more narrowly regarded the *DNB* as recording the past achievements of 'the British and Irish race'; 'A Statistical Account', pp. xxii and x.

[53] Qoted in Smith and Elder's contemporary advertisement for the completed *DNB*, together with matching revolving bookcase.

[54] Robert Faber and Brian Harrison, 'The *Dictionary of National Biography*: A Publishing History', in *Lives in Print: Biography and the Book Trade from the Middle Ages to the 21st Century*, ed. Robin Myers, Michael Harris and Giles Mandelbrote (2002), p. 172.

[55] Sidney Lee, 'Memoir of George Smith', *DNB*, vol. xxii (*Supplement*) (1909), p. xlv; Lee, 'A Statistical Account', p. xxii; *Oxford DNB*, vol. li, p. 182.

The *DNB* avoided presenting itself as a work of moral edification. As Lee said, it was, 'first and foremost, a work of historic reference', what we would call a scholarly resource.[56] Yet its very selectiveness inevitably implied that prominence was better than obscurity, distinction superior to mediocrity. Many of its life stories testified to the value of industry, self-reliance and creativity. Though supposed to be written in a non-judgemental way, the articles were by no means free from moralising. Besides, it was assumed that facts would speak for themselves. Stephen said that the writer should 'not pronounce a panegyric upon heroism, but he ought so to arrange his narrative that the reader may be irresistibly led to say "Bravo!"'[57] The Supplements contain lives of civil servants, written by other mandarins, which are essentially hymns to the virtues of diligent, un-self-regarding public service.[58] But then, can a life story ever be other than exemplary?[59] How

[56] Sidney Lee, 'At a Journey's End', *The Nineteenth Century and After*, 72 (1912): 1157.
[57] Stephen, 'National Biography', *Studies of a Biographer*, vol. i, p. 23.
[58] Gently lampooned by David Cannadine, 'British Worthies', *London Review of Books*, 3 (3–10 Dec. 1981): 3.
[59] Peter France, 'From Eulogy to Biography: The French Academic *Eloge*', in *Mapping Lives*, ed. France and St Clair, p. 100.

can it help being a stimulus to reflection, emulation or avoidance? How can we learn to live, save by observing the lives of others?

The earlier biographical compilations, from which the *DNB* drew most of its names, were heavily biased towards literary figures, partly because they were written by literary people, partly because authors of published works always have an advantage in the immortality stakes. When the *DNB* was being planned, one contemporary declared that 'every man and every woman who has written a book must be included', and a reviewer of the early volumes took it for granted that three quarters of the space 'is and must be taken up by the lives of authors'.[60] According to A. F. Pollard, a sub-editor on the *DNB*, when a name came up for possible inclusion, Lee's first question was 'what did he write?'[61] Hence the inclusion of such minor authors as the early Victorian orientalist Stephen Reay, of whom we are told that he was mild and ineffectual in character, but 'remembered by colleagues with affection for his

---

[60] H. S. Ashbee, in *The Athenaeum*, 2880 (6 Jan. 1883), p. 17; (R. C. Christie), review of *DNB*, vols. i–x, in *Quarterly Review*, 328 (1887): 374.

[61] A. F. Pollard, 'Sir Sidney Lee and the "Dictionary of National Biography"', *Bulletin of the Institute of Historical Research*, 4 (1926–7): 10.

habits of pottering around the library in search of his spectacles and hovering over hot-air gratings in search of warmth'.[62] Yet Stephen's *DNB* also included a wide range of other occupations. The highly inclusive style of the late eighteenth-century compilations fitted in well with his own belief that the most valuable part of a dictionary was its lives of 'the second-rate people'.[63] Lee, a Balliol man, was more establishment minded and moved nearer the idea of the *DNB* as a kind of '*Who Was Who*', asserting that 'the life of a nonentity or a mediocrity, however skilfully contrived, conflicts with primary biographic principles' and that 'no person deserves a biography unless he be, in the literal sense, distinguished'.[64] 'From the year 1000 AD to the end of the present century', he informed a lecture audience in 1896, 'some 30,000 persons who have lived and died in this kingdom have achieved such measure of distinction as to claim the national biographer's attention ... at the present moment [and here the purr of his listeners

---

[62] *Oxford DNB*, vol. xlvi, p. 244.

[63] Stephen, 'National Biography', *Studies of a Biographer*, vol. i, p. 21.

[64] *Principles of Biography* (Leslie Stephen Lecture, Cambridge, 1911), p. 10; *The Perspective of Biography* (English Association, 1918), p. 7. The difference between the two men is noted by Jane Marcus, *Auto/Biographical Discourses: Theory, Custom, Practice* (Manchester and New York, 1994), pp. 97–8.

becomes audible], there are in the city of London about 600 adult persons qualifying for admission.'[65] By a person of distinction, Lee meant someone 'who by virtue of a combination of character and exploit has arrested contemporary attention and is likely to excite the curiosity or interest of a future generation'.[66] The number of such persons, he explained, would vary from one period to another; the eighteenth century, for example, had been too peaceful to offer opportunities to achieve distinction comparable to those enjoyed by the people who lived through the 'stupendous crises' of the sixteenth and seventeenth centuries.[67]

The Supplements to the *DNB*, published by Oxford University Press at regular intervals through the twentieth century, were on a smaller scale than the original venture. As a result, their editors found that, after including the great and the good, there was no room left for anyone else, even if they had wanted anyone else, which is unlikely. Theirs was a metropolitan and 'establishment' view of who and what mattered. The lives were written within a few years of the subject's death,

---

[65] Sidney Lee, 'National Biography' (lecture at the Royal Institution), *Cornhill Magazine*, new ser., 26 (1896): 271–3.

[66] Lee, *The Perspective of Biography*, p. 7.

[67] Lee, 'A Statistical Account', pp. xiii–xiv.

often with the widow and children looking over the contributor's shoulder. They resembled the additions to the *Biographia Britannica*, of which Horace Walpole remarked that they were 'partial and flattering, being contributions of the friends of those whose lives are recorded'.[68] Contemporaries have personal knowledge of a kind inaccessible to later historians, but they are also more discreet. Dr Johnson believed that only those who had known a man at close quarters could write his life, but he also thought it wrong to cause unnecessary pain to the deceased's friends and relatives; as a result, 'what is known can seldom be immediately told; and when it might be told, it is no longer known'.[69]

During the twentieth century, many countries produced new dictionaries of national biography, the most ambitious being the excellent Italian one, which began publication in 1960 and has so far taken sixty-one volumes to reach the letter 'J'. At home, works like the *History of Parliament* and Howard Colvin's *Biographical Dictionary of British Architects* transformed areas which were traditionally the *DNB*'s business. Others, more

---

[68] *The Letters of Horace Walpole*, ed. Mrs Paget Toynbee (Oxford, 1903–18), vol. xi, p. 122 (5 Feb. 1780).

[69] *Boswell's Life of Johnson*, vol. ii, pp. 79, 116, 446; Samuel Johnson, *Lives of the English Poets* (World's Classics, 1906), vol. i, p. 438 (Life of Addison).

menacingly, offered a radically different biographical canon. The *Dictionary of Welsh Biography*, the *Dictionary of Business Biography*, the *Dictionary of Labour Biography* and the *Biographical Dictionary of British Feminists* each constituted a frontal assault upon the *DNB*'s hegemony. Who wanted the old *DNB*, now that there were specialised biographical dictionaries on every subject, from colonial governors to racehorse trainers in Berkshire?[70] The world of professional scholarship had expanded, the volume of source material had multiplied, historical attitudes had changed, and Stephen's creation looked increasingly out of date.

This was the background to the decision in 1992 by the Oxford University Press and the British Academy, backed by an augmented government grant, to produce a new version. Thanks to the clear vision of the founding editor, Colin Matthew, the determination of his successor, Brian Harrison, the commitment of the editorial and project staff led by Robert Faber, the labours of 10,000 contributors scattered across the world (over 370 of them alive and living in Cambridge), the

---

[70] Anthony Kirk-Greene, *A Biographical Dictionary of the British Colonial Governor* (Brighton, 1980); Daniel Boyd, *A Biographical Dictionary of Racehorse Trainers in Berkshire* (Reading, 1998).

advantage of new technology, and the huge generosity and financial buoyancy of Oxford University Press, the project has now been published on the exact date agreed eleven years ago.

Like its predecessor, the *Oxford DNB* has conducted its labours in the full light of day.[71] Lectures, interviews and newsletters have kept the world so well informed that, even before publication, many people already had a good idea of how the new version would differ from the old. Even without reading the informative 'Introduction', they knew that 63 per cent of the old lives have been rewritten and the remainder revised; that there are over 16,000 new lives; that the number of women included has more than trebled; that the categories of business and labour have nearly doubled; that there is increased coverage of foreign visitors and of inhabitants of British territories overseas; that there is fuller treatment of Roman Britain, pre-independence America and twentieth-century Britain; that there are 10,000 authentic likenesses; that the contributors are mostly specialists on their subject, whereas over half of the old *DNB* was written by thirty-four people; that a capacious list of sources is appended to every entry; and

---

[71] Lee, 'A Statistical Account', p. v.

that the temporary absence of an index is more than made up for by the astonishing search facilities which accompany the on-line version. (Here is a dimension of the *Oxford DNB* which has no precedent. It is hard to think of *any* aspect of the British past which will not be illuminated by running a word search of this colossal database.) Finally, it is known that the text will be regularly corrected and augmented on-line, so that its obsolescence can be indefinitely deferred.

All this has been done in so pragmatic and commonsensical a way that it seems faintly inappropriate to scrutinise the *Oxford DNB* for its philosophical underpinnings. Besides, Matthew's decision to include in the new version all the names to be found in the old one, however inconsequential, has meant that the result is a hybrid, a Burkean amalgam of past, present and, in its on-line version, future. As at a royal garden party, where politicians and captains of industry jostle with district nurses and lollipop men, so the footballers, comedians and pop musicians introduced by Matthew and Harrison find themselves rubbing shoulders with the literary and clerical luminaries favoured by Stephen and Lee. This is a very different philosophy from that of the *American National Biography* of 1999, which discarded the selection made in the older *Dictionary of American Biography* and started afresh; or of Madame Tussaud's waxworks, which ejects its exhibits when their moment of fame has passed. There has been no 'depantheonisation' in the *Oxford DNB*.

With 10,000 contributors, all encouraged to display their authorial individuality,[72] the work can hardly reflect a single outlook. No choir as gigantic as that can sing harmoniously and the song sheet never intended them to. Just as Stephen found high churchmen to write about high churchmen, and Baptists to write about Baptists, so Matthew and Harrison give us Simon Heffer on Enoch Powell and Eric Hobsbawm on Karl Marx. One could say of the *Oxford DNB* what F. W. Maitland said of its predecessor: it can fairly claim to be national, if only because it reflects the confusion of the national mind.[73]

Yet though individual contributors may reveal their sympathies, the project as a whole is intended as a neutral work of reference, with no political or moral message. If asked about its purpose, the makers of the

---

[72] In his *Editor's Annual Report* to the Supervisory Committee (Apr. 1995), Matthew stressed the importance of maintaining 'the individuality of approach so desirable in a reference work which, despite all the high tech, records one person's view of another' (p. 5).

[73] Frederic William Maitland, *The Life and Letters of Leslie Stephen* (1906), p. 368.

*Oxford DNB* do not use the language of the *Biographia Britannica*: they say nothing about piety to ancestors or national honour or the need to set good examples before posterity. The publicity materials talk freely of 'heroes' and 'villains', but there is little suggestion in the *Dictionary* itself that its lives are in any way exemplary. The subjects have been chosen for their historical importance. Studying them will satisfy our curiosity and enhance our understanding. But there is no implication that it will make us morally better or more patriotic.

The theme of nationality is very muted. With the accelerated migration of people, the European Union, globalisation of trade and communications, and internationalisation of science, sport and entertainment, the membership of a single nation state is now a less all-defining matter than it used to be and the national identity of many individuals is increasingly elusive. The nation state itself seems an artificial and fragile construction.

In these circumstances, the *Oxford DNB* takes an even broader view of nationality than did Leslie Stephen. At the planning stage, the project was described in-house as 'an authoritative record of national achievement'; the government grant to get the scheme under way was secured by the plea that the work was 'of considerable national importance'; and the Prince of Wales has said that he hopes that the *Oxford DNB* will teach future generations to 'appreciate the UK's seminal cultural impact'.[74] Yet Colin Matthew believed that, as nationality gave way to European citizenship, so would reference books; he even envisaged the eventual aggregation of national dictionaries into a single world biography. The *Oxford DNB*'s view of nationality had, therefore, to be 'fluid, practical and inclusive'.[75] The resulting work, which includes lives of Julius Caesar, Erasmus, Handel, Washington, Marx and Gandhi, can hardly be accused of being narrowly nationalistic (though a critic might detect in such catholicity a kind of 'lexicographical irredentism',[76] which turns a disproportionate share of the world's most notable figures into honorary Britons).

[74] 'A Second Edition of the *Dictionary of National Biography*' (May 1990) (Oxford University Press archives); British Academy, Bid to DES for Financial Year, 1992–3 (British Academy archives); Prince of Wales's congratulatory message, read at the launch of the *Oxford DNB* in the National Portrait Gallery, 29 Sept. 2004.

[75] Colin Matthew, 'Dictionaries of National Biography', in *National Biographies and National Identity*, ed. Iain McCalman, with Jodi Parvey and Misty Cork (Canberra, 1996), p. 17; and *Leslie Stephen and the* New Dictionary of National Biography, pp. 35–7.

[76] I lift this expression from Elizabeth Baigent, 'Nationality and Dictionaries of National Biography', in *National Biographies and National Identity*, ed. McCalman, p. 64.

Yet the *Oxford DNB* is far from indifferent to the problems of nation-building which have preoccupied other compilers of national biography. Its greater attention to Wales, Scotland, Ireland and the English provinces reflects current anxieties about fissiparous tendencies within the UK. Its concern to include more women, business people, icons of popular culture and recent immigrants reveals a desire, not just to understand the past, but also to provide a charter for a present which is democratic, gender-neutral, ethnically and culturally diverse. Prominent figures in the history of Africa, the Far East and the Caribbean are included; and well over 10 per cent of the new entrants from the twentieth century were born outside the British Isles.[77] As with the old *DNB*, the implication is that these heterogeneous individuals are all somehow part of a single inheritance, a culture which we all share. Even so, there must be embarrassment about the fact that 2000 is too early a closing date for the *Dictionary* to reflect the changes in British society brought about by post-1945 immigration. Has Dr Johnson's servant the ex-slave, Francis Barber, been included because he was historically influential or because it was thought important to provide some

[77] Alex May, 'Nationality in the *DNB*; the Modern End', *Oxford DNB Newsletter*, 6 June 2001.

forebears for the black citizens of modern Britain, who as yet are still relatively invisible?

The *Oxford DNB* has also tried to modify the individualist assumptions implicit in any biographical dictionary. Sidney Lee believed that a biographer should state 'the facts and characteristics that distinguish a man from other men'; and the old *DNB* was essentially 'a dictionary of individuals very individually handled'.[78] It did not assert that Great Men made history, or even that history was the sum of innumerable biographies, but the reader could have been forgiven for thinking so.

A century later, when few historians regard Great Men as the motor force of historical change,[79] the *Oxford DNB* seeks to show the constraints to which individual achievement is subject and to reveal it as usually the result of collective activity, in which many others, now forgotten, were also involved. The entry on Alexander Fleming of penicillin fame is scathing about 'the Fleming myth, of a lone scientist making

---

[78] Lee, 'National Biography', p. 265; Colin Matthew, *Editor's Annual Report* to the Supervisory Committee (Apr. 1993), p. 9.

[79] See, e.g., the remarks of Sir Ian Kershaw in the Preface to his *Hitler 1889–1936: Hubris* (Harmondsworth, 1998), p. xxi; and in *Times Higher Education Supplement*, 16 Jan. 2004, p. 23.

a chance discovery that allowed infectious diseases to be conquered'; while that on the Victorian philanthropist, William Rathbone, remarks that 'the conventions of biography seek to isolate individual contributions, but many of Rathbone's projects were collaborative'.[80] The exploits of military leaders, artists, inventors and business entrepreneurs are also scaled down by this approach. So are those of dictionary editors, for, just as the credits at the end of a modern film offer a seemingly endless list of gaffers, best boys and other production assistants, so the opening pages of the *Oxford DNB* call a long roll of consultant editors, associate editors, research staff, publishing staff, research associates, freelance, temporary and part-time staff, without whom the work could never have been accomplished.

Sidney Lee claimed that, in the *DNB*, 'No sphere of activity has been consciously overlooked. Niches have been found for sportsmen and leaders of society who have commanded public attention. Malefactors whose crimes excite a permanent interest have received hardly less attention than benefactors.'[81] The criteria for the *Oxford DNB* are not very different, but they have been more

---

[80] *Oxford DNB*, vol. xx, p. 37; vol. xlvi, p. 105.
[81] 'A Statistical Account', p. x.

resolutely applied. The editors do not talk of 'distinction' any more, but of 'influence – whether for good or ill'.[82] Whereas Lee was suspicious of the 'evanescent repute' achieved by 'journalistic iteration', declaring that 'current fame is no sure evidence of biographic fitness',[83] Matthew and Harrison have no compunction about including media-created 'celebrities' and 'personalities'. John Lennon gets as much space as Henry Purcell; Princess Diana rather more than Mary Wollstonecraft; William Millington, the first Provost of King's, slightly less than his namesake, Mary Millington, pornographic star of *I'm Not Feeling Myself Tonight*. This is a reversion to the principle enunciated in 1799 by John Aikin in his *General Biography*: 'Fame, or celebrity, is the grand principle upon which the choice of subjects for a general biography must be founded.'[84] The implication is that there is no single hierarchy of achievement. Different occupations and activities are equally valid, equally of interest.

Within each occupation, however, there is still a hierarchy: the *Oxford DNB* abounds in judgements, carefully calibrated and eminently disputable, of the kind

---

[82] *Oxford DNB*, vol. i, p. viii.
[83] Sir Sidney Lee, *Elizabethan and Other Essays* (1929), p. 39 (repeating his *Principles of Biography*, pp. 16–17).
[84] Aikin, *General Biography*, vol. i, Preface, p. 2.

which gives Handel 12½ pages, Britten 12, Elgar 8½, Walton 6½, and Purcell 6¼; or, coming near home, 1 to George Kitson Clark, 1½ to David Knowles, 3 to Herbert Butterfield, 4½ each to Lord Acton and G. M. Trevelyan, 5 to Geoffrey Elton and 5¾ to Maitland.[85] Yet the gap between top and bottom is narrower than it used to be. There is none of that mixture of obsequiousness and commercial acumen which led Lee to give 50,000 words to Edward VII and 93,000 to Queen Victoria, so that the articles could be spun off as freestanding biographies.

Concise biographies, which can be quickly grasped and assimilated, inevitably have the effect of scaling down their subjects and making them seem less formidable.[86] Moreover, ours is supposedly an anti-heroic age. Since Marx, Freud and Lytton Strachey, biography has become irreverent and subversive. We know that human beings are imperfect and we suspect the motives which underlie exceptional achievement. The *Oxford DNB* is acutely aware of the extent to which reputations are constructed, by the subjects themselves, by the media and by posterity.

---

[85] Of course, some of these differences in length reflect the varying reactions of contributors to the editorial instructions, rather than the instructions themselves.

[86] Cf. Claude Lévi-Strauss's remarks on miniatures in *The Savage Mind* (English trans., 1966), p. 23.

The old *DNB* stated simply that Joshua Reynolds was 'the greatest portrait-painter that England has produced'. The new one accepts that Reynolds was the most innovative portrait painter of his day, but also stresses his personal ambition, his use of patronage and social networks, and his 'extraordinary desire to channel his energies into gaining public recognition'.[87] The entry on Winston Churchill concludes that Churchill was conscious of 'the importance of imagery in politics and his image was no less important in establishing his fame than his speeches'.[88]

Most recent national biographies have shown a similar anti-heroic, democratising tendency. The *Neue Deutsche Biographie* reduced Bismarck from over 200 pages to 8½. The *Dictionary of Welsh Biography* aimed at 'a representative selection, illustrating the whole history of the Welsh people of all social classes, at all periods and in all walks of life ... The question of intrinsic merit does not arise.'[89] The *Dictionary of Canadian Biography* included 'workers, craftsmen, farmers, fishermen', on the grounds that 'these humble people deserve their chronicles', no less than politicians or artists; and the *American*

[87] *Oxford DNB*, vol. xlvi, p. 564.
[88] *Oxford DNB*, vol. xi, p. 684.
[89] *The Dictionary of Welsh Biography down to 1940* (1959), p. xv.

44

*National Biography* deliberately makes room for 'a few persons of admittedly ephemeral significance', 'to show how they were representative of American popular culture at a given moment in the country's history'.[90]

In its inclusion of more women, the *Oxford DNB* also reflects the spirit of the age. In 1662 Fuller thought that the mothers of his worthies deserved mention for the way in which they educated their sons.[91] But in the old *DNB*, that so-called phallocentric monument,[92] the subjects frequently had no mothers; and wives, if mentioned, normally appeared only at the end of the article. In the early Supplements the subjects were children of a father *by* a mother. Only from 1950 were they children of a father *and* a mother. Women accounted for only 4 per cent of the lives in the old *DNB*, and not all of them had their own entries. Even Sarah, Duchess of Marlborough appeared as an appendage to her husband's life.[93]

[90] *Dictionary of Canadian Biography*, vol. x, p. xi; 1st *Supplement* to *American National Biography*, ed. Paul Betz and Mark C. Carnes (New York, 2002), p. vii.

[91] Fuller, *Worthies*, vol. i, p. 10.

[92] Jane Marcus, in *Virginia Woolf: A Feminist Slant*, ed. Jane Marcus (Lincoln, NE, 1983), p. 11.

[93] As was noted by the *English Historical Review*'s anonymous reviewer (presumably the editor, Mandell Creighton) of the first 22 volumes of the *DNB*; *English Historical Review*, 5 (1890): 786–7.

Sidney Lee calculated in 1896 that women's opportunities at that time to achieve what he regarded as distinction were one in thirty of those of men.[94]

The *Oxford DNB* has raised the proportion of female subjects to 10 per cent. It has been able to do so because of the greater public role of women in the twentieth century and because more attention has been given to women's role in earlier periods in such activities as nursing, lay religious work and charity, which the old *DNB* did not regard as part of the public sphere. It also gives more space to those women who seem more important now than they did in the 1880s. Aphra Behn's entry is over three times as long as the old one, and Lady Rachel Russell moves from fifteen words to three and a half pages. If Shakespeare had had a sister Judith, as Virginia Woolf famously imagined, we may be confident that Colin Matthew would have put her in. He believed that women had been more influential in the public life of the past than the *DNB* implied. But he accepted that, unless household management and child-rearing qualified for inclusion, there was no way of ever getting them up to

[94] Lee, 'National Biography', p. 273. This closely accords with the calculation that, of the 28,201 lives in the *DNB* and its three Supplements of 1901, the separate articles on women totalled 998; Gillian Fenwick, *Women and the* Dictionary of National Biography (Aldershot, 1994), p. 6.

parity.[95] The group articles, on such subjects as women Lollards or women agents in occupied France, are well intentioned, but they raise the question of why there are no equivalent pieces on their male counterparts. The real task is to ascertain and express the role played by wives, mothers, sisters, daughters and servants in what historians write up as the story of a man's career, but which, more often than not, was a joint enterprise.

In the second edition of the *Biographia Britannica*, the entry on Archbishop Atherton, executed in 1641 for sodomy, was omitted, for reasons of delicacy. The old *DNB* had similar inhibitions, observing with painful imprecision that Oscar Wilde was convicted of 'offences under the Criminal Law Amendment Act'. The *Oxford DNB* claims to eschew euphemisms about sex, illegitimacy, alcohol and mental illness; and its inclusion of the subject's wealth at death, removes, however imperfectly, another ancient taboo. But it still sometimes uses the laconic formula, 'he never married', to mean more than it says;[96] and the on-line search

---

[95] Colin Matthew, 'British History, Research and the *D.N.B.*' (unpublished paper of 1993), p. 10.

[96] The excellent article on Sidney Lee, a 'lifelong bachelor' who repudiated his original, 'literal' reading of Shakespeare's *Sonnets* in the wake of the Oscar Wilde trial, leaves the reader with the clear impression that he was a repressed homosexual, but avoids directly saying so.

facility reveals eighty-eight people who did not suffer fools gladly (as well as one who did). The closer the *Dictionary* gets to the present day, the more cautious it becomes, unless the target is a safe one, like Robert Maxwell, who is baldly characterised as 'publisher and swindler'.

The inclusion of 10,000 authenticated likenesses, the 'the largest "curated" collection of national portraiture ever assembled',[97] is essentially a return to an older tradition. Collections of *Viri Illustres* or *Icones*, combining a portrait with a brief biographical description, were a familiar Renaissance genre, like cabinets of portrait medals or libraries decorated with portrait friezes and busts.[98] In the eighteenth century, so-called 'catalogues of English heads'[99] and the likenesses in Granger's *Biographical History* intensified the fashion for collecting portrait engravings as visual exemplars of the British past. The Cornish MP, Richard Bull, put together an

[97] Brian Harrison, *New DNB: Editor's Annual Report* to the Supervisory Committee (May 2001), p. 10.

[98] See, e.g., Francis Haskell, *History and its Images* (New Haven, CT, and London, 1993), chap. 2; T. C. Price Zimmermann, *Paolo Giovio: the Historian and the Crisis of Sixteenth-Century Italy* (Princeton, NJ, 1995), pp. 206–8, 282; *Modelling the Individual*, ed. Enenkel *et al.*, pp. 23–4; André Masson, *The Pictorial Catalogue: Mural Decoration in Libraries* (Oxford, 1981).

[99] E.g., Thomas Birch, *The Heads of Illustrious Persons of Great Britain* (1743–51); Joseph Ames, *A Catalogue of English Heads* (1748).

extra-illustrated copy of Granger, containing some 14,500 portraits, rather more than the *Oxford DNB*, though, of course, not authenticated; Scottish portraits were collected in John Pinkerton's *Iconographia Scotica* (1797) and *The Scottish Gallery*, or *Portraits of Eminent Persons of Scotland* (1799); while Sir William Musgrave, who died in 1800 (and unfortunately does not appear in the *Oxford DNB*), formed a huge collection on British biography from manuscript and visual material, including records of nearly 8,000 painted portraits.[100]

The *Dictionary*'s reunion of biography and portraiture lacks the rationale provided by the ancient belief that physiognomy reveals character in a way that other sources cannot, because the face mirrors the soul. Rather, it arises from Leslie Stephen's conviction that outward appearance was part of a subject's individuality, a biographical fact like any other.[101] Some of the new portraits

[100] Arline Meyer, 'Sir William Musgrave's "Lists" of Portraits; with an Account of Head-Hunting in the Eighteenth Century', *Walpole Society*, 54 (1988); Antony Griffiths, 'Sir William Musgrave and British Biography', *British Library Journal*, 18 (1992); Lucy Peltz, 'Engraved Portrait Heads and the Rise of Extra-Illustration: the Eton Correspondence of the Reverend James Granger and Richard Bull, 1769–1774', *Walpole Society*, 64 (2004), p. 7.

[101] Colin Matthew, *Editor's Annual Report* to the Supervisory Committee (Apr. 1993), p. 7; *New Dictionary of National Biography: Notes for Contributors* (corrected reprint, 1998), p. 2.

powerfully evoke the immediacy of the individual presence. They record dress and period style; and they will help to identify other likenesses of the person illustrated. But I suspect that their real function is to satisfy the reader's curiosity, just as photographs of authors are now *de rigueur* in a publisher's catalogue. They also encourage such undisciplined reflections as Virginia Woolf's belief that you could tell from Mary Wollstonecraft's face, 'at once so resolute and so dreamy, so sensual and so intelligent', that her life 'was bound to be tempestuous'.[102]

To literary theorists, worried by epistemological concerns about identity and the stability of the self, the lives in the *Oxford DNB* may appear to impose a spurious coherence and linearity on what was fragmented and unconsecutive. The contributors are sensitive to the limitations of the surviving evidence, especially the medievalists, who make much use of 'perhaps', and 'may have' and 'it seems'. But few are inhibited by post-modern scepticism about the very possibility of objective biography. Neither do they engage in psychological speculation. Havelock Ellis, who believed that human beings were crucially shaped by experiences in the womb, thought that the old *DNB*, in place of 'genuine biography', offered 'slices

[102] 'Four Figures, iii: Mary Wollstonecraft', in *The Common Reader*, 2nd ser., (new edn, 1935), p. 159.

of mis-placed history';[103] and, in a sense, he was right. The new *DNB* is not much more concerned than the old one with its subjects' inner psyche; there is more about private life than there used to be, but essentially it offers narratives of public careers. It betrays few signs of the eighteenth-century belief that biography is the raw material for the science of human nature. Yet one cannot read these lives without hugely enhancing one's sense of the range of human possibility.

The old *DNB* did not immediately change the way people viewed the British past. But it did suggest an infinity of new insights. The interpretative revolution associated with Sir Lewis Namier was predicted by Sidney Lee as early as 1896, when he remarked that biography gave the historian a better understanding of 'the vicissitudes of party government in the eighteenth century' by revealing 'all the ties of kinship or of early friendship which brought political colleagues together [and] ... the domestic rivalries which drove politicians into opposing camps'.[104]

Who can tell whether the *Oxford DNB* will stimulate similar revolutions in historical perception? History is

---

[103] Havelock Ellis, 'An Open letter to Biographers', in *Views and Reviews: A Selection of Uncollected Articles, 1884–1932, 1st Series 1884–1919* (1932), pp. 88, 91–2.
[104] Lee, 'National Biography', p. 263.

concerned with general trends, of which life stories can at best be no more than illustrative. That is why some critics dismiss biography as intrinsically anti-intellectual, an evasion of larger issues.[105] Yet most of us retain faith in the importance of human agency, however constricted the circumstances in which it has to operate. We also know that the story of individual experience reveals the complexity of the historical process and provides a salutary check on easy generalisation. The *Oxford DNB*'s short lives can be more informative than full-volume biographies, because their outlines are clearer; their authors focus on essentials and, unlike some writers of full-scale biography, they have to decide what those essentials are. These new lives embody the enormous volume of research and reinterpretation which has accumulated over the past hundred years. To compare them with those they replace is to receive an intensive course in modern historiography.[106] There is no better way of

---

[105] Terry Eagleton, 'Knock-Me-Down Romantic', *London Review of Books*, 25 (12) (19 June 2003), p. 7. In his entry on Colin Matthew, Ross McKibbin observes that 'the writing of national histories via individual biographies went against historiographical developments, both in Britian and abroad', *Oxford DNB*, vol. xxxvii, p. 340.

[106] Changes in the treatment of the medieval lives are discussed by Henry Summerson, 'Problems of Medieval Biography: Revising *DNB*', *Medieval Prosopography*, 17 (1996).

catching up with whole tracts of current scholarship than by reading the new entries on, say, W. B. Yeats or Charles Darwin or Oliver Cromwell or Edward the Confessor or Thomas Hobbes or so many others.

There is a tendency nowadays to suspect the motives behind any outwardly philanthropic act and to ask what is really going on. Surely the Oxford University Press and the British Academy cannot have spent over £25 million, just to produce a work of scholarly reference? What is the unstated agenda? Is this a bid by a group of academics for cultural hegemony — an attempt to ensure that they are the owners of the past, the gate-keepers controlling admission to the temple of fame? Some modern critics have denounced the old *DNB* as the sinister attempt of late Victorian liberal intellectuals to consolidate their cultural power.[107] There is some truth in this charge, in so far as the *DNB*, like its predecessors, laid heavy emphasis on literary and intellectual achievement. But the *Oxford DNB* is so all-embracing,

[107] David Amigoni, 'Life Histories and the Cultural Politics of Historical Knowing: the *Dictionary of National Biography* and the Late Nineteenth-Century Political Field', in *Life and Work History Analyses: Qualitative and Quantitative Developments*, ed. Shirley Dex (*Sociological Review* Monograph 37, 1991); and Amigoni, *Victorian Biography: Intellectuals and the Ordering of Discourse* (Hemel Hempstead, 1993), p. 180 n. 27.

and its nomination process so open, that it is hard to believe that the outcome serves any sectional interest, other than the reputation of the British Academy and Oxford University Press. In any case, the *Dictionary* has no monopoly of the past. It is but one reference work among many. Its authors have little prospect of controlling popular memory, even if they wanted to.

Indeed, since the *Oxford DNB* is necessarily only a selection of past lives, it is bound to seem an anomaly in a populist age. Ironically, the more people it includes, the harder it becomes to justify the exclusion of the remainder. In 1939 Leslie Stephen's daughter asked why only the great should have their lives recorded: 'Is not anyone who has lived a life and left a record of that life worthy of biography – the failures as well as the successes, the humble as well as the illustrious? And what is greatness? And what smallness?'[108]

Virginia Woolf's scepticism is famous. It recalls Johnson's belief that there is no one whose life is not worth recording. It is less well known that Leslie Stephen himself came near to disowning the intellectual foundations on which his great edifice had been reared. In his *Science of Ethics* he stated that society was an organic

---

[108] Virgina Woolf, 'The Art of Biography', in *The Death of the Moth and Other Essays* (Harmondsworth, 1961), p. 168.

growth and that its nature could not be inferred from the character of the individuals who composed it.[109] In his essay, 'Forgotten Benefactors', he declared that advances were not achieved by individuals, but by general movements of opinion. He stressed the accidents of reputation which made some persons immortal and consigned others to oblivion. Most people were easily replaceable: 'there must have been countless forgotten Newtons and Descartes'. Fame was capricious and misleading; and there was no objective test by which absolute merit could be assessed. The greatest benefactors of mankind were persons who lived in obscurity, 'whose very names will soon be forgotten, and who are entirely eclipsed by people whose services, though not equally valuable, are by their nature more public'.[110] Here surely was an echo of the last lines of *Middlemarch*: 'the growing good of the world is partly dependent on unhistoric acts; and that things are not so ill with you and me as they might have been is half owing to the number who have lived a hidden life, and rest in unvisited tombs'.

[109] *The Science of Ethics* (1862), p. 31.

[110] Leslie Stephen, 'Forgotten Benefactors', in *Social Rights and Duties: Addresses to Ethical Societies* (1896), vol. ii, pp. 230, 246. He expressed similar sentiments (provoked in both cases by thoughts of his late wife, Julia) in *Sir Leslie Stephen's Mausoleum Book*, ed. Alan Bell (Oxford, 1997), p. 96.

Now that historians concern themselves with all sections of past populations, there is in principle no reason why many of these hidden lives should not be recovered; and there is no technological obstacle to storing them electronically. One day perhaps we may have a database so vast that its claim to be a true national biography will be incontrovertible. Meanwhile, in the *Oxford DNB*, we have a magnificent collaborative achievement and, in its publication, a literary event of the highest importance.